Intelligent Jokes

Intelligent Jokes

compiled by
Sion Rubi

Manic D Press
San Francisco

Originally published in Hebrew by Or-Am Publishers, Israel.

Cover design: Scott Idleman/BLINK

ISBN 0-916397-97-1

Note: Many of these jokes have been in circulation for years and we have been unable to verify the original authorship

Foreword

The joke is a literary genre: an unsophisticated interpretation of the short story form. As in every field of art, jokes are categorized according to the consumers' degree of intellect. There are jokes that are more appropriate for people with a certain modicum of intelligence. This book is intended for those people.

Written in a colloquial style of speech, the jokes sound as if someone were telling them, so that they appear on the page in a natural state. The jokes are not divided by topic. In life, events don't occur according to subject matter. Sometimes a joke may remind a person present at its telling of another joke about the same subject, and that's the way it is in this book.

When you, the reader, are in a bad mood or are just restless, bored, and debating whether to open the refrigerator and eat something even though you're not hungry; or turn on the television even though earlier you decided that there's nothing interesting to watch; or light a cigarette if you smoke – all just to keep yourself busy with something – instead, take this book and read a little. You'll achieve the same goal of keeping yourself busy, except it will be *good* for your health.

Sion Rubi
Jerusalem, Israel

A man meets his friend after he hadn't seen him in twenty years. He says to his friend, "You look terrific! What do you do to look so good?"

The friend says, "Look, I have one rule. I don't argue with people."

The man says, "How can it be from that?!"

The friend says, "You're right, it couldn't possibly be from that."

☺

A man tells his wife, "You know, I don't feel like going to the Robinsons' party."

She replies, "I don't feel like going either, but imagine how happy they'll be if we don't go."

☺

A ninety-year-old man goes to an insurance company and asks for life insurance.

The clerk says, "I'm sorry, but at your age we don't give insurance."

The man says, "What do you mean? My father's still alive."

The clerk says, "If your father's still alive, that's another story." The clerk goes to the manager to consult with him. He comes back and tells the man, "Come back on Tuesday at ten o'clock and we'll give you insurance."

The man says, "I can't come on Tuesday, my grandfather's getting married then."

The clerk asks, "How old is your grandfather?"

The man says, "He's 136."

The clerk says, "He's 136 years old and still wants to get married?"

The man says, "No, he doesn't want to get married but his parents are pressuring him."

☺

Two gentlemen go to a restaurant and order fish. They receive two fish on one plate. Each of them has to help himself to a fish. One of the fish is smaller than the other. Each of the men knew that if he takes his fish first, good manners require that he take the smaller one.

One says to the other, "Please go ahead!"

The other says, "You help yourself first, please."

This continues three or four times, each one urging the other to take his fish first. After a while one of them got tired of arguing and he took the larger fish.

The other says, "That's not very nice. You helped yourself first *and* you took the larger one."

The first one says, "What would you have done?"

The second one says, "I would have taken the smaller one."

The first one says, "Good, so you got the smaller one!"

☺

A bald man, standing next to his house that is going up in flames, has his hands in his pockets as if he's playing with something there.

His friend passes by and says, "I see that your house is burning down. Why are you standing like an idiot with your hands in your pockets? If I were you I'd be pulling my hair out!"

The bald man says, "That's what I'm doing."

☺

A man goes to visit his friend in a different city. The man tells his friend how good it is to live in the city he came from and brags about how healthy he is.

The friend replies, "When I came here I had no hair on my head at all. Now my head is full of hair."

The man is amazed and says, "How did that happen?"

The friend says, "I was born here."

☺

When the first astronaut landed on the moon, three aliens were taking a morning stroll.

When they saw the astronaut, one of them says to his friend, "Look at that strange creature. It's not alive but it's moving."

☺

Three astronauts – an Englishman, a Frenchman and a Jew – return from a trip into space.

The space station's doctor examines them and says, "You caught an incurable disease and within a month your willy will stop functioning."

The astronauts are asked what they would like to do during this month.

The Englishman says, "I want two ladies, a bottle of whiskey and two pounds of veal steak every day."

He's told, "No problem, you'll get everything you asked for."

The Frenchman says, "I want a beautiful girl, two bottles of champagne and three pounds of excellent French cheese every day."

He's told, "No problem, you'll get everything you asked for."

They ask the Jew, "What do you want to do during this month?"

The Jew replies, "I'd like to see another doctor."

☺

A man standing in line at a telephone booth loses his patience.

He goes into the booth and tells the man on the phone, "I see you've been holding the phone for fifteen minutes without speaking."

The man answers angrily, "Sir, would you excuse me? I'm talking to my wife!"

☺

A man says to his wife, "You used to tell me that I mean the world to you."

She says, "That's true, but meanwhile I learned a little geography."

☺

A guy asks his girlfriend, "Would you marry someone even if he weren't rich?"

She says, "Of course. What's important is that he's calm and easygoing."

He asks, "Even if he doesn't have money?"

She says, "A person who doesn't have money can't be calm and easygoing."

☺

A person enters the pharmacy and asks the pharmacist, "Sir, do you have anything against mosquitoes?"

The pharmacist says, "I personally don't have anything against mosquitoes."

☺

A shrewd salesman is sitting on the train eating small fish. He collects the fish heads in a jar. Across from him sits a naive farmer who asks him, "What are you saving those fish heads for?"

The salesman says, "Don't you know? Whoever eats these fish heads gets brains."

The farmer says, "Oh well, sell me some."

The salesman sells him some for $10. The farmer starts to eat one and suddenly he thinks, 'I could have bought all of those fish with the heads for $10.' He says to the salesman, "You tricked me."

The salesman says, "You see, you only ate one and you're smarter already."

☺

A guest arrives in Jerusalem to visit a friend who was a very religious man. The friend tells his guest about the War of 1948, and about how much danger Jerusalem was in.

The guest asks, "How was the city saved?"

The friend says, "The City was saved thanks to two things, one action and one miracle."

The guest asks, "What was the action?"

The friend says, "The action was that we sat and read the Book of Psalms for three days."

The guest asks, "Then what was the miracle?"

The friend replies, "The miracle was that the army arrived in time."

☺

A wife's husband passed away. The funeral was beginning. The street was narrow. On the corner of the street the coffin hits a wall and the deceased awakens and stands up.

Ten years later, he dies again.

When the funeral begins, the wife says to the pallbearers, "Be careful at the corner."

☺

A girl who has reached maturity places a personal ad in the newspaper that says that she's seeking a partner who is tall, brave and a real man.

Two days later a man arrives who's six feet tall with both hands in a cast, and says, "I am here to answer the ad."

The girl says, "I can see that you're tall, and I think I can also see that you're brave. Both of your hands are in a cast, so it looks like you've done something brave. Now, what about being a man?"

The man says, "You see that I can't use my hands."

She says, "True."

He says, "What do you think I rang the doorbell with?"

☺

A team of civil engineers invented a computer that can answer every question. A group of army generals came to check out the computer.

One general asks the computer a question.

The computer answers, "Yes."

He asks another question and the computer answers, "Yes."

And so it continues for the third question, the computer again answers, "Yes."

The general gets angry and says to the computer, "Can you say anything else besides 'yes' all the time?"

The computer answers, "Yes, sir!"

☺

A divorced woman consults with her divorced friend and says, "I have two marriage candidates. I love one of them but he's poor. The other is wealthy."

The friend says, "Love is eternal. Marry the one you love."

The woman says, "I think I will."

Afterwards the friend says, "And why don't you give me the wealthy one's phone number?"

☺

A man goes to the doctor complaining of weakness. The doctor examines him and says, "When you were a baby you didn't get enough breastmilk."

The man asks around to find out where he can get breastmilk.

A female neighbor hears the story and tells him, "Come visit me, I'll give you breastmilk."

He goes to her and she lets him suck her breasts. She gets aroused and wants to move on to a more intimate stage.

She says to him, "Maybe there's something else that you want?"

The man says, "Yes, do you have a cookie?"

☺

A man that died arrives in heaven. They balance his sins and good deeds and decide to send him to hell. A week later they take him out and put him in heaven. Three days later they send him back to hell.

The man asks the angel that escorts him, "Why are you driving me crazy? What's going on here?"

The angel says, "Well, according to the balance of your sins and good deeds, we put you in hell. When you were in hell your son donated $10,000 to his church, so we took you out and brought you to heaven. But three days later the check bounced. We had to take you back to hell."

☺

A ranch owner from Texas comes to visit his farmer friend in Israel. The friend takes him for a tour of his farm from one end to the other.

After the tour is over, the Texan says, "You know, on my ranch I start the tour with my car at nine in the morning and get to the other end at one o'clock."

The Israeli says, "I used to have a piece of junk like that but I sold it."

☺

A woman tells her friend, "I saw you yesterday with your husband. He looks good in his new suit."

The friend says, "What new suit?"

The woman says, "He looks totally different."

The friend says, "That was my new husband."

☺

When Michael was younger, he just hated going to weddings. All of his uncles and aunts used to come up to him, poke him in the ribs, giggle, and say to him, "You're next, Michael."

But they stopped doing that after Michael started doing the same thing to them at funerals.

☺

A young man was struggling with the question, 'What is life?'. He looked in philosophy books. Their answers didn't satisfy him. He went to the clergy but their answers didn't satisfy him. He kept looking, when finally he was told that there was an old wise man that had found the answer, living in a hut on a tall mountain in north India. The man went to India. After many hardships he found the Indian wise man. He asks the wise man, "My great teacher, tell me, what is life?"

The wise man looks at the man with a fatherly gaze, raises his hand, and says, "Son, life is like a river. . . everything flows, everything changes."

The young man says, "How can that be? How can life be compared to a river?"

The Indian wise man is shocked and says, "So life isn't like a river?"

☺

A husband tells his wife that he wrote in his will that he is leaving all his property to her on the condition that she marry another man immediately after he passes on.

She says, "Darling, how could I do that? I'll be in mourning. Why did you request that?"

He says, "Well, then I'll be sure that at least one person will mourn for me."

☺

In the morning, when a husband was about to leave for work, his wife gives him a small package.

He asks, "What's this?"

She says, "Hair conditioner."

He asks, "What do I need this for?"

She says, "It's not for you, it's for your secretary. Her hair sheds all over your clothes."

☺

A man is walking down the street and sees a funeral. He comes closer and notices his friend among the escorts. He asks his friend, "What's going on? Whose funeral is it?"

The friend says, "My wife's."

The man asks, "How can that be? Your wife died two years ago."

The friend says, "I remarried."

The man says, "You remarried? Congratulations!"

☺

A girl tells her friend that she's sad because her boyfriend left her.

Her friend says, "You shouldn't be sad, time is the best healer."

The girl says, "Maybe it's a good healer but it's not a beauty specialist."

☺

A nightclub hostess complains to her friend that she's being charged high taxes.

The friend says, "Don't worry. Pay the taxes with a smile on your face."

The hostess says, "I'm willing to, but they want cash."

☺

In an American school, a teacher asks his pupils, "Who is the most famous man in the world?" and adds, "Whoever knows the answer will win a prize."

One pupil raises his hand and says, "George Washington."

The teacher says, "Washington is famous but mainly in America."

Another student raises his hand and says, "Abraham Lincoln."

The teacher says, "Lincoln is famous too but mainly in America."

A Jewish boy raises his hand and says, "Jesus."

The teacher says, "That's right! You win a prize."

After class, the teacher approaches the Jewish pupil and asks him, "How is it that you said Jesus and not Moses? For you, he's more famous."

The Jewish child replies, "Moses is Moses and business is business."

☺

A tourist gets on a bus and gives the bus driver a $10 bill. The bus driver gives him a ticket and $19 change. The man goes in and sits down.

Suddenly the bus driver remembers and says to the man, "Hey, how much did you give me?"

The man says, "$10."

The driver asks, "And how much change did you get?"

He says, "$19."

The driver asks, "And why didn't you say anything?"

The man says, "How am I supposed to know what your prices are?"

☺

An eighty-year-old man goes to the doctor and complains that he can't have intercourse like he used to.

The doctor says, "My friend, it's a matter of age. At your age it isn't easy."

The man says, "What do you mean? I have a friend who is two years older than me who tells me that he has intercourse twice a week."

The doctor says, "Okay, so go tell everyone that you do, too."

☺

A very religious man arrives in Paris and wants to visit a nightclub.

The guard says, "I see by the way you're dressed that you're a religious man. This place isn't for you. We have girls here that perform barefoot from head to toe."

The man says, "I know, I want to go in."

The guard says, "As long as you understand, then please, go right ahead in."

The man sits next to a table. The lights are dimmed and a stripper gets on the stage and begins to strip. Suddenly the man begins to shout, "I can't see it, I can't see it."

The guard goes over to him and says, "But I told you what they show here, why are you shouting now?"

The man continues to shout, "I can't see it."

The manager comes and asks the man, "Is it true that you were told what you would see here?"

The man says, "Yes, I was told."

The manager says, "Then why are you shouting that you can't see it?"

The man says, "I can't see it, the pole is in my way."

☺

A statistician riding the train sees a large herd of cows through the window. Across from him sits a cowboy.

The statistician says to the cowboy, "I wonder how many cows there are in that herd."

The cowboy takes a look at the herd and says, "84."

The statistician is amazed at the cowboy's ability to count that fast and asks him, "How could you have counted so fast?"

The cowboy says, "It was simple. I just counted the legs and divided them by 4."

☺

A physics teacher tells his class about light substances and asks, "Who can give an example of a light substance?"

One pupil raises his hand and says, "The willy."

The teacher asks, "How is that?"

The pupil says, "A simple thought is enough to raise it."

Then the teacher begins talking about heavy substances and asks, "Who can give an example of a heavy substance?"

The same pupil raises his hand again and says, "The willy."

The teacher asks, "How is that?"

The pupil says, "If it doesn't rise, no power in the world can lift it."

☺

A man asks his friend, "You're always telling me that you're afraid of your wife, so how is it that yesterday she came to you on all fours?"

The friend says, "She was looking for me under the bed."

☺

A woman goes to a lawyer to consult with him about a divorce because her husband never keeps the house organized.

The lawyer asks her, "Did you try everything to convince him to keep the place neat?"

The wife says, "Of course! Not one plate in the kitchen is still in one piece."

☺

God decided to bring a flood to the world. He informs the heads of three religions a week in advance.

The Pope calls out to his believers and asks that everyone confess his sins.

The Imam in Mecca asks his believers to do a lot of charity deeds.

The Chief Rabbi suggests to his believers that they make all preparations necessary to live on water.

☺

Two young men who had graduated from college together, one with a degree in economics and the other with a degree in psychology, meet a year later on the street. The psychologist is driving a Chevy.

The economist asks, "I see that you bought a car already. How did you do that in just a year?"

The psychologist says, "I work in a bank. I got promoted and I'm a department manager. Psychology, my friend. And what about you?"

The economist says, "I work here and there but I spend my money on beer."

A year later they meet again. This time the psychologist is driving a Lexus and the economist is still walking. The economist asks, "How did you do it?"

The psychologist answers, "Yeah, I got promoted and now I'm a division manager. Psychology, my friend." And he asks, "What's up with you?"

The economist says, "I work here and there but I buy cases of beer."

A year later they meet again and this time the economist is driving a Mercedes. The psychologist asks, "How did you do it? You said you were only working here and there and buying cases of beer with all your money."

The economist says, "That's true, but last week I cashed in the empty bottles."

☺

A woman goes to the doctor to consult with him about her husband's talking in his sleep.

The doctor says, "I'll give you some medicine to make him stop talking."

The woman says, "That's not the problem. I want you to give me medicine to make him speak more clearly."

☺

A mother asks her daughter, "I see that this man has been dating you for a long time. Why don't you marry him?"

The daughter says, "I enjoy his courting so much that I don't want to lose it."

☺

A woman goes into a store to buy a purse. She asks the price for various purses. Finally she finds a small purse that she likes. She asks the store manager, "How much does it cost?"

The manager says, "$200."

The woman says, "Why is it so expensive?"

The store manager says, "My dear woman, this is a multi-purpose purse. It's made out of an elephant's organ. When necessary, you caress the purse, it grows and can be used as a suitcase."

☺

A stingy husband passes by a steakhouse with his wife while taking a walk.

The wife says, "Wow! The steak smells great."

The husband says, "You're right, it does smell great. Let's walk by there again!"

☺

A couple sits on a bench on a summer night. Silence.

She asks him, "What are you thinking about?"

He says, "The same thing you're thinking about."
She says, "You're very vulgar."

☺

A man goes to the police station and says to the officer, "I want to talk to the thief that broke into our house."

The officer asks, "For what purpose?"

The man says, "I want to know how he was able to get into our house after midnight without waking my wife."

☺

A man visits his friend and notices that he's not with his wife.

He asks him, "Where's your wife?"

The friend says, "She left me during a fight. I said a few harsh words to her."

The man says, "I'm sorry to hear that... Maybe you remember what words you said?"

☺

A man is standing at a train station and overhears a conversation between two young men.

One of them, "Thanks for your hospitality, everything was terrific. The room, the food, and your wife was great in bed."

After one departs the man says, "Did I hear correctly that you told your friend that his wife was great in bed?"

He replies, "That's right. The truth is that his wife wasn't so great but he's a good friend of mine and I didn't want to hurt his feelings."

A couple was planning to marry.

The man asks his girlfriend, "Honey, do you think you'll be able to get along with my salary?"

The girlfriend says, "I will, but what will you live off?"

A man asks his friend, "Have you ever seen a lie detector machine?"

His friend replies, "What do you mean have I seen one? I'm married to one."

A woman tells her friend that a 250-pound burden was lifted from her.

The friend says, "How do you know that it's exactly 250 pounds?"

The woman says, "I divorced my husband."

☺

A man finds a rabbit in the street. A friend of his passes by and sees the man holding the rabbit in his arms. He says to him, "What's this?"

The man says, "I found her in the street."

The friend says, "Bring her to the zoo."

The next day the friend meets the man again and sees that the man is still holding the rabbit in his arms. This time the rabbit's wearing a bathing cap and sunglasses.

The friend says to him, "I thought I told you to take her to the zoo."

The man says, "Yesterday I took her to the zoo, today she wants to go to the beach."

☺

An elderly couple, the man is 90 years old and the woman is 80, go to get a divorce.

The clerk asks them, "What made you decide to get a divorce at your age?"

The old couple says, "We've been wanting to get a divorce for a long time but we felt uncomfortable because of the children, so we waited for the children to die."

☺

A miser used to go to the Western Wall in Jerusalem every Thursday to put a note between the stones with a request: *God, let me win a million dollars in the lottery.* This continued for a whole year. Finally the angel Gabriel said to God, "Look, this fellow has been coming every Thursday with the same request for a whole year. Maybe we can do something for him?"

God replied, "I agree, but let him buy a lottery ticket first."

☺

An unemployed glasscutter says to the village fool, "Go break some windows in a few buildings so that I'll have some work, and I'll give you something for it."

The fool goes and breaks all the windows in the glasscutter's house.

The glasscutter says, "What have you done? I meant other people's houses."

The fool says, "Look, if I had broken windows in other people's houses, they might have gotten another glasscutter to fix them, but in your house I knew for sure that you would fix them and then you'd have work."

☺

A driver stops next to a policeman on a busy square in town and asks the policeman, "Am I driving okay?"

The policeman says, "Drive, drive, I didn't say anything to you, you're delaying the traffic."

The driver drives around the block, comes back, and asks the policeman, "Aren't I driving okay?"

The policeman says, "Yes, yes, drive, drive."

The driver says, "Then why don't they want to give me a driver's license?"

☺

A couple that got married makes an agreement that if they ever cheat on one another they will put a bean in a box for every betrayal. Forty years later they decide to open the boxes. In the husband's box they find three beans, and in the wife's box there are no beans at all.

The husband asks, "How can this be? There was one incident that you confessed to yourself. Tell me the truth."

The wife says, "Okay, if you want to know, I'll tell you. Remember once, late at night, you wanted bean soup? Where could I have gotten you beans at that hour of the night?"

☺

A man meets his friend after he hasn't seen him for thirty years. He says to him, "You look terrific, what did you do to look so good?"

The friend says, "When I got married forty years ago I made an arrangement with my wife. Every time I yell at her, she goes into the kitchen, closes the door and I'm not allowed to go in there. And every time she yells at me, I go out to the balcony, close the door, and she's not allowed to come out there. Since then, I've spent two-thirds of my marriage out on the balcony in the fresh air."

☺

A charity institute arrived at an agreement with a fundraiser that if he raises money for the institute, half the money would go to the institute and the other half to him. A few months later the fundraiser gets a phone call from the institute and they ask him, "What's up with the money?"

The fundraiser says, "I've hardly raised my half."

☺

A married woman invites her lover to her house. While they're in bed they hear the husband's footsteps in the hall. The wife says to the lover, "Hurry, jump out of the window."

The lover says, "Are you crazy? We're on the 13th floor!"

The woman says, "Hurry, now is not the time to be superstitious."

☺

A man tells his friend, "My wife lives in constant fear that her expensive clothes will be stolen."

The friend says, "How do you know?"

The man says, "Yesterday I came home unexpectedly. I open the closet and I see a man standing there. I ask him, 'What are you doing here?' He says that my wife hired him to guard her clothes."

☺

A religious young man confesses to the rabbi, "Rabbi, I sinned, I kissed a girl."

The rabbi says, "If you kissed her on the face, the Lord will forgive you."

The young man says, "I kissed her lower down."

The rabbi says, "If you kissed her on her bellybutton, the Lord will also forgive you."

The young man says, "I kissed her even lower down."

The rabbi says, "Even if you kissed her on her knees, the Lord will forgive you."

A business owner to whom one of his customers owed money and his requests for payment didn't help, writes to her one day, *Ma'am, what will your neighbors think if one day they come and confiscate your television?*

The woman replies, *Sir, I checked out the subject with my neighbors. They think that it's an idiotic idea.*

A husband goes out to spend his day off fishing. He comes home in the evening and shows his wife all the fish he caught.

The wife says, "Don't brag, the neighbor saw you in the fish store."

The husband replies, "You see how many fish I caught? I caught so many that I had to sell some to the fish store."

☺

A fortune-teller says to a new client, "A visit with me costs $20. For that amount, you can ask two questions."

The client says, "Isn't that a lot of money for two questions?"

The fortune-teller says, "You're right, it is too much. Now what's your second question?"

☺

During an auction, the auctioneer announces to the audience that one lady lost her purse and she's willing to give $100 to whoever finds it. From the back of the room a voice calls out, "$120!"

☺

The owner of a bed factory tells his friend that while visiting a nightclub, he met a pretty dancer. Because he didn't know her language, they communicated through drawings.

When he drew a couple dancing, she understood and got up to dance with him.

Then he drew a taxi and she nodded in agreement.

Afterwards she draws him a bed.

He asks his friend, "Tell me, how did she know that I manufacture beds?"

☺

A mother says to her young daughter, "Last night I heard that you had a boy with you in your room. What do you know about him?"

The daughter says, "Nothing."

The mother says, "But I heard you calling him 'darling.' "

The daughter says, "Yes, that's because I couldn't remember his name."

☺

A man who broke into the same dress store four times in one night is brought before the judge.

The judge asks him, "What did you steal from the store?"

The man says, "Just one dress."

The judge asks, "Then why did you break into the same store four times?"

The man says, "My wife sent me back three times to change it."

☺

A priest tries to comfort a woman whose husband died suddenly.

He tells her, "This must be terrible for you."

The woman says, "Yes, it is. Now I have to wear black and I don't look good in black."

☺

A comedian gets on stage.

He tells the audience, "It's now 9:00 and my program will last for an hour."

Someone from the audience asks, "What comes after your program?"

The comedian says, "10:00."

☺

There were two neighbors. One was an indifferent non-religious person and the other was anti-religious who would always curse God. After they both had died, the non-religious one was sent to hell and the anti-religious one to heaven.

The non-religious one says to the angel, "How could this be? At least I didn't curse God."

The angel says, "Your neighbor who cursed God at least believed that he exists."

☺

A man goes into a club to apply for membership.

The clerk asks him, "How old are you?"

The man says, "Fifty."

After a year, he leaves the club. Four years later, he comes back to apply for membership to the club. The clerk asks, "How old are you?"

The man says, "Fifty."

The clerk says, "How is that possible? Five years ago you said you were fifty."

The man says, "You see that I don't lie. I said the same thing then, too."

☺

A circus puts an ad in the newspaper looking for a man that can do it six times in an hour. A man answers the ad and says that he can. During the show the man does it three times, four times, and hardly makes it to five times.

The manager says, "But we agreed on six times."

The man says, "But you didn't tell me about the rehearsal in the morning."

☺

A priest asks one of his congregation members how his wife is.

The husband wonders, "Why, sir, are you asking about my wife?"

The priest says, "Yesterday at church she was coughing very loudly."

The husband says, "Don't worry, yesterday she came to church wearing her new hat."

☺

A young woman married a wealthy man.

Her mother says to her, "I would have preferred that you didn't marry such a wealthy man."

The daughter says, "Don't worry, Mom, soon he won't be so wealthy."

☺

A woman who was married for twenty years says to her husband, "One day let's do it on a public park bench."

The husband says, "Have you lost your mind?"

The wife insists and says, "I want to feel young again."

Finally he agrees.

During the act a policeman catches them and writes two tickets: $50 for the woman and $100 for the husband.

The wife asks, "Why do I get only $50 and he gets $100?"

The policeman says, "It's your first time, but I've caught him a few times already."

☺

A rabbi and a Catholic priest ride a train together. The priest takes out ham sandwiches and offers one to the rabbi. The rabbi says, "You know that we can't eat ham."

The priest says, "You don't know what you're missing."

A few seconds later the rabbi says, "Your wife made you the sandwiches?"

The priest says, "You know we're not allowed to marry."

The rabbi says, "You don't know what you're missing."

☺

A man goes to visit a madhouse. In the courtyard he sees one of the patients working in the garden, digging and watering in a correct manner. Next to him stands someone who's helping him and telling him how to do the work.

The visitor says to the guide, "I see that this man is working well like any other person, why does he have to be kept in an institution?"

The guide says, "That's true. The problem is that he thinks that he's King Solomon."

The man says, "What does that matter? The main thing is that he works okay."

The guide says, "That's true. The problem is that I'm King Solomon and there can't be two."

☺

A woman says to her husband, "Every time you see a pretty girl, you lose your head and forget that you're married."

The husband replies, "On the contrary, when I see a pretty girl that's when I remember that I *am* married."

☺

A liberal father gives his grown-up daughter a guidebook about sexual relations with men.

After a while he asks her, "So, did you read the book?"

The daughter says "Yes, and I also wrote the author with a few corrections and additions."

☺

A woman tells her friend that she married her first husband for his money, divorced him, and married her second husband for love.

The friend said, "That is an ideal arrangement."

The woman says, "Not really. The problem is that my first husband married me for love and my second husband for my money."

☺

A man says to his friend's wife that he would like to go to bed with her one time.

The woman says, "I'm faithful to my husband. I won't do anything like that."

The man says, "What if I give you $1,000?"

The woman says, "A thousand dollars is another thing. Come tomorrow morning when my husband isn't home."

The man comes, does what he does, and leaves $1,000.

Her husband comes home in the evening and asks, "Was my friend here today?"

The wife says, "Yes."

The husband asks, "Did he leave $1,000?"

The wife says, "Yes. How did you know he left $1,000?"

The husband says, "He really is an honest person. Yesterday he borrowed $1,000 from me and said that he'd give it back today."

☺

A knight who went on a distant journey puts a chastity belt on his wife and gives the key to his friend.

The next day, while resting at the first station, his friend comes up to him urgently and says, "The key doesn't fit."

The knight says, "You're telling me?"

☺

A man who thought he was a mouse was admitted to hospital for treatment.

After being there a month the doctor asks him, "You know now that you're not a mouse, right?"

The man says, "Right."

The doctor says, "Okay, you can go home."

The man leaves, arrives at the hospital gate, and sees a cat next to the gate. He runs back to his doctor.

The doctor says, "But you know now that you're not a mouse."

The man says, "It's true I know, but I'm not sure that the cat knows."

☺

A boy asks his father, "Tell me, Father, do donkeys get married?"

The father replies, "Only donkeys get married."

☺

A young woman tells her friend that she called off her engagement with her boyfriend.

Her friend asks, "Did you give him back the gold watch that he gave you as a gift?"

The young woman says, "Of course not, my feelings for the watch haven't changed."

☺

A boy asks his girlfriend, "Tell me, what do you prefer, a good-looking guy or an intelligent guy?"

The girlfriend says, "Neither, I prefer you."

☺

A man invites his friend to visit him at home.

The friend asks, "How do I get there?"

The man says, "You take the bus until the last stop, get off and walk straight about 100 feet, then you'll see a white house with a green iron gate, open the door with your elbow and come in."

The friend asks, "Why should I open the door with my elbow?"

The man says, "Well, you don't intend to come empty-handed, do you?"

☺

A man goes into the barbershop with a boy.

After the man finishes getting his haircut, he tells the barber, "Now cut the boy's hair too, I'll be back soon."

When he's finished cutting the boy's hair, the barber asks him, "When is your father coming back to pay?"

The boy says, "He's not my father. He met me in the street and asked if I wanted a free haircut."

☺

A husband says to his wife in bed, "Did you ever feel like being a man?"

The wife says, "No, never, what about you?"

☺

A Jewish grandmother is sitting on the beach with her granddaughter. Suddenly, a big wave comes and sweeps the girl away.

The grandmother says, "God, what have you done to me? She is such a sweet girl and she hasn't done anything wrong. Please bring her back to me."

A few seconds later another big wave comes and brings the girl back to the shore safe and sound.

The grandmother says angrily, "And where is her hat?"

☺

A guy whose girlfriend came from a respected family is invited to their house for dinner. He sits down and their dog comes over and sits on his lap. The guy is very nervous and stressed. From all the excitement, his food gets stuck in his throat and he starts to hiccup.

After the first hiccup, the girlfriend's mother calls out the dog's name, "Maxi!"

After the second hiccup, the mother calls out again, "Maxi!"

The guy is pleased that the mother thinks that it's the dog that's hiccuping.

After the third hiccup the mother calls out, "Get down, Maxi, in another minute he'll puke on you."

☺

A farmer visits a big city for the first time and goes into a café and orders coffee.

The waitress asks him, "What kind of coffee?"

The farmer who isn't familiar with different kinds of coffee says to her, "What kinds do you have?"

The waitress says, "We have latte, capuccino, and espresso."

The farmer says, "Give me an espresso."

The waitress returns with a tiny cup of espresso.

The farmer drinks the small cup in one gulp and says to her, "It's okay, bring me a cup of that."

☺

A beggar says to a fancy lady, "It's been three days since I've tasted food."

The lady replies, "I wish I had that kind of self-control."

☺

On their wedding night the bride asks the groom, "Tell me, how many women have you gone to bed with before me?"

He is silent.

After a minute of silence, she asks him, "Are you angry?"

He says, "No, why? I'm still counting."

☺

A man meets a pretty waitress and starts dating her. After a while he decides that he wants to marry her. But he has reservations concerning her past. He hires a detective to investigate. A month later he gets a report saying that there's nothing wrong with her past, but lately she's been seen with a man with suspicions concerning his past.

☺

Two partners go to the rabbi to rule on a dispute between them.

First, one of them comes and tells his version. The rabbi says, "You're right."

The next day the partner comes and tells his version. The rabbi says, "You're right."

The rabbi's wife says to the rabbi, "How can both of them be right?"

The rabbi says to her, "You're also right."

☺

A modern version of the previous joke:

Two partners go to a modern rabbi to rule on a dispute between them. First one comes and tells his version.

The rabbi says, "As far as I can see from what you've told me, your partner's right. But wait, don't lose hope. Tomorrow your partner is coming to see me. Maybe from what he says I'll see that you're right."

☺

Frank, Sam, and Henry always met once a week to discuss the world's situation. On one occasion, they tried to solve the problem of life.

"What is the problem of life?" asked Henry.

The more they talked about it, the more they thought they knew the answer. The problem of life is that everyone has worries.

"If people didn't have any worries," said Sam, "then life would be easy."

But now that they knew, another question remained: How can we three end our worries?

They thought for a while and then Frank said, "Why don't we hire somebody to do all the worrying for us so that we can then have it easy?"

Sam said, "Great idea. It wouldn't be easy, I know, but between us, we could pay him well to make up for the difficulty of the role."

So they all agreed to chip in to pay someone $5000 a month to do all their worrying for them.

They were very happy with this decision until Sam pointed out the flaw.

"Tell me," he said, "if a man is making $5000 each month, what has he got to worry about?"

☺

A woman from high society goes to get her picture taken by a famous photographer. A few days later she comes to get the pictures.

She looks at the pictures and says to the photographer, "They don't look as good as last time."

The photographer says, "My dear woman, take into consideration that I've grown twenty years older since then."

☺

A new lady in the neighborhood goes to visit her neighbor.

When it was time to depart, the neighbor says to her son, "Come, Evan, give our new neighbor a kiss."

Evan says, "I don't want to. Daddy tried to yesterday and got smacked."

☺

A state governor visits a prison. He passes from man to man and asks each one why he was arrested. All of them say that they're not guilty and that they're doing time because of a mistake. Only one prisoner admits that he stole. The governor orders that the prisoner be released and says, "A thief shouldn't be amongst so many honest people. He's liable to corrupt them."

☺

A man goes to the barber for a shave. While he's being shaved the barber's dog sits and looks at them.

The man says to the barber, "I see your dog enjoys watching you shave."

The barber says, "That's not the reason. Sometimes a piece of ear falls off."

☺

A man orders dinner in a restaurant.

When he's finished he says to the waiter, "I'm sorry, I left my wallet at home."

The waiter says, "That's okay. I'll write your name on the wall next to the cash register and when you come back, you can pay."

The man says, "But it's not nice that everybody can see my name."

The waiter says, "Nobody will be able to read your name because your coat will be hanging over it until you return."

☺

A mother who took her son to the doctor is arguing with him about the bill.

"Isn't this excessive, asking for so much money for treating the measles? You forget that my son's had 14 visits here."

Then she adds, "And you forget that he infected his whole class."

☺

A guy says to his friend, who is known to be a cheapskate, "I heard that you made up with your girlfriend, and that you're getting married after all."

The friend says, "Well, my girlfriend gained weight and couldn't get the engagement ring off her finger."

☺

A Romanian bicycle rider visits Washington. He parks his bike next to the Internal Revenue Service building and wants to leave it there.

A policeman comes over to him and says to him, "What are you leaving your bike here for? Don't you know that this is the IRS building?"

The Romanian says, "It's okay, I locked the bike."

☺

A religious man is walking on the street and sees a pretty girl with a low neckline.

The devil whispers to him, "Look how stimulating she is. The pleasure could be even bigger than heaven."

The man closes his eyes and tries to think other thoughts, but the devil doesn't leave him alone.

In the end he says to the devil, "Okay, you've convinced me. Now go and convince her."

☺

A woman is standing next to a window in her apartment and is chatting with her neighbor who's standing on the balcony next door with her young daughter.

Suddenly the neighbor says, "I can see your husband coming with a bouquet of flowers."

The woman says, "Oh, I see that tonight I'll have to spread my legs."

The little girl says to her mother, "Mommy, why does she have to spread her legs? Don't they have a vase?"

☺

Two brothers are sitting in a room playing. Suddenly the phone rings in the other room.

The older brother says to the younger one, "Go see who it is."

The little brother goes to the other room, looks around and comes back.

He says, "There's nobody there, it's just the telephone ringing."

☺

Two anthropologists visit a remote area in Mexico. One day both their watches stop. In the distance they see an old farmer sitting and dozing next to his horse. They go up to him and ask, "Do you know what time it is?"

The old man doesn't move. He extends his cane, uses it to lift the horse's tail to a certain angle and tells them the time. They were astonished at how he was able to know the time from the angle of the horse's tail.

Two hours later they return and ask again, "What time is it?"

The old man again tells them exactly what time it is in the same manner.

They ask him to reveal the secret and are willing to pay for it.

The old man says, "See, it's very simple. Up there on the church tower, there's a clock. The horse's tail is in my way. I lift up the tail and I can see the clock."

☺

A guest arrives at a family when they were just about to begin their meal. The master of the house says to the guest, "Come eat with us."

The guest says, "I just ate at home."

The master of the house pleads with the guest and finally the guest agrees and says, "I'll taste something."

They bring the guest a full plate and he finishes it. They bring him another full plate and he finishes it as well. There almost wasn't enough food left for everyone.

When the guest is about to leave, the master of the house says, "Next time, taste something at home and come eat with us afterwards."

☺

A woman goes shopping at a well-known household goods and furniture store with her little boy. She leaves the boy in the store's playroom. When she's done shopping, she goes back to get her son but the boy's enjoying himself so much, he doesn't want to leave the playroom.

She tries to convince him to come with her but nothing helps. The boy doesn't want to leave. She goes over to the young man who is supervising the children and asks for his advice.

The young man says, "I'll convince him."

He goes over, and whispers something in the boy's ear. The boy immediately runs to his mother and is willing to leave.

The woman is amazed at how the counselor succeeded so quickly in convincing the boy. She asks the playroom supervisor to tell her what he said to the boy. The young man refuses, but in the end, gives in.

He says, "I told the boy that if he doesn't leave, I'll break his bones."

☺

A guy stands next to the rail on a ship. A girl is standing not to far away. The guy wants to hit on her.

He says to her, "The sea is rough today."

The girl says, "I can't hear you."

The guy says in a louder voice, "The sea is rough today."

The girl shouts, "It's hard to hear you, the sea is rough today."

☺

A fair-haired chambermaid worked in a small hotel. A guest arrives and suggests that she sleep with him the next day.

She does it but asks, "How did you know I would agree?"

The guest says, "It's written in the Bible."

A few days later another guest arrives. He too suggests the same to her and he too says, "It's written in the Bible."

The same happens with a third guest. She decides to open the Bible and see what's written there. She sees that on the first page someone wrote, *The blonde one puts out.*

☺

Two children, a brother and sister, would visit their grandmother every weekend. The grandmother would ask them what good deed they did this week. They would tell her about the good deed and she would give each a gift. One weekend, the grandmother asks, "What good deed did you do this week?"

The brother says, "This week I helped an old lady cross the street."

The grandmother asks the girl, "What good deed did you do this week?"

The girl says, "I helped my brother cross the street with the old lady because she didn't want to."

☺

A boy didn't speak until he was 12. They were sure he was mute. Once they sat at the table for a meal, suddenly the boy says to his neighbor, "Please pass the salt."

Everyone was astonished that he could speak. They ask him, "How come you never spoke until now?"

The boy says, "Until now I was given everything without having to ask."

☺

An Englishman buys a horse and hires porters to take the horse up to his apartment on the fourth floor. The porters exert themselves and sweat. Finally they succeed in getting the horse to his apartment.

He asks them to put the horse in the bathtub.

After they finish the job, one of the porters asks him, "Why do you need a horse in the bathtub?"

The Englishman says, "Well, tomorrow evening I'm having a party at home. One of the guests will go into the bathroom, see the horse, come to me and say, 'You know you have a horse in your bathtub.' And I'll tell him, 'So what?' "

☺

A married woman liked to go to the amusement park and ride the ferris wheel.

One day, her husband says, "Be careful that no one sees your underwear."

She says, "Okay."

When she gets back, he asks her, "So were you careful that nobody saw your underwear?"

She says, "Of course. To be one hundred percent certain I took them off before I got on."

☺

When Napoleon went on his victory journey, every place he went had bells ring in his honor. One day he arrived at some town and the bells didn't ring. When the mayor came to greet him, Napoleon asks him, "Why didn't the bells ring in my honor?"

The mayor says, "Emperor, sir, we have seven reasons why the bells didn't ring. First, we don't have any bells."

Napoleon stops him there and says, "That's enough."

☺

There was a man who, when he would take off his shoes at night, would throw them at the wall across from him. On the other side of the wall lived a neighbor.

One evening, the neighbor comes to him and asks him not to throw his shoes at the wall because it disturbs him.

The next day the man takes off his shoes, and out of routine he throws the first shoe at the wall. Then he remembers the neighbor's request and lays down the other shoe quietly on the floor.

Half an hour later, the neighbor comes knocking on his door and says, "Damn it, go on and throw the other shoe already."

☺

In a small town, a search was on for a new rabbi for the local synagogue. Two candidates arrive and are lodged at the same hotel in adjoining rooms. One was a scholar and the other was a crook that knew how to make an impression.

The test was that each had to give a sermon at the next upcoming Sabbath services. The scholar wrote a sermon and rehearsed it in his room out loud. The crook heard the scholar's sermon and wrote it down word for word and learned it by heart.

When the time comes on the Sabbath for the sermon, the crook asks to go first, and gives the scholar's sermon. The scholar's turn arrives.

The scholar goes up to the pulpit and says, "Members of the congregation, as you know anyone can prepare a sermon. I will now demonstrate my memory's unusual capability. I will repeat my predecessor's sermon word for word."

☺

A future father-in-law asks the guy that wants to marry his daughter, "If I give you a large dowry, what can you give me in return?"
The son-in-law says, "I can give you a receipt."

☺

A girl asks her mother, "Where did you meet Daddy?"
The mother says, "At a picnic."
The girl says, "Did I go there with you?"
The mother says, "No, sweetheart, only on the way back."

☺

A mother puts her daughter to sleep and tells her, "When you pray, mention your grandmother, that God should give her a long life and good aging."

The daughter says, "Grandma is already old enough. It's better that I ask God to make her younger."

☺

A traffic officer is about to write a ticket for a driver that didn't signal when he made a left turn. Suddenly he hears the wife yelling in the back seat, "I told you to be careful, you never listen to me. You're always getting into trouble when you drive. I'm glad they caught you."

The officer asks, "Who is that?"

The driver says, "That's my wife."

The officer says, "You can go, my friend, you have been punished badly enough."

☺

Two burglars come out of a bank after they took their loot in a sack.

On the way, one says to his friend, "Let's count how much money we took."

The friend says, "That's a waste of time. If we wait until morning we can read exactly how much we took in the newspapers."

☺

Two movie stars are walking on the street.

Suddenly one of them says to his friend, "Wow! Look at that! Across the street my wife and my mistress are walking together."

The friend says, "I was about to tell you the same thing."

☺

A man moves to a different city because of his work. He tells his neighbor that he came to live an honest and decent life here. The neighbor says, "That should be easy, you won't have many competitors here."

☺

A man wandering at night under suspicious circumstances is stopped by a cop.

The cop asks him, "Do you have a job?"

The guy says, "Sometimes I do and sometimes I don't."

The cop asks, "Where do you work?"

He says, "Here and there."

The cop says, "Come with me to the police station."

The guy asks, "And when will I get out of there?"

The cop says, "Sooner or later."

☺

A guy asks a girl he recently met, "How old do you think I am?"
She says, "How should I know? You look young for your age."

☺

A guy says to his friend, "That's it, I'll never be able to ask another girl to marry me."
The friend says, "Why? Did she refuse you again?"
He says, "No, she agreed to marry me."

☺

A man staying in a hotel asks the receptionist for an envelope.
The receptionist asks, "Are you a guest here?"
The man says, "No way, I'm paying $200 a night."

☺

An annoying woman asks a soldier with a bandaged leg, "How were you hurt?"
The soldier says, "By a shell."

The woman asks, "Did it blow up?"

The soldier says, "No, it crawled under the table and bit me."

☺

A movie actress meets a guy during a flight. When they get off the plane he asks here if he can go out with her that evening. She says, "I can't, I'm getting married tonight. Maybe tomorrow?"

☺

A girl asks her friend, "What kind of husband would you recommend that I choose?"

The friend says, "Forget about the husbands, get yourself an available man."

☺

A woman tells her neighbor, "My husband was the first man who kissed me."

The friend says, "Are you boasting or sorry?"

☺

A son asks his father, "Did Edison invent the talking machine?"

The father said, "No, son. God invented the first talking machine and Edison invented an improved talking machine that can also be stopped."

☺

A mother gives advice to her innocent daughter who was about to go out on her first date with a boy. She says to her, "Whatever he asks you to do, even a small kiss, say 'No.' "

When she gets back home, her mother says, "I saw through the window that you kissed the boy."

The daughter says, "He asked me if I would mind if he kissed me. I said, 'No.' "

☺

A woman says to her friend's husband, "I heard from your wife that you haven't spoken to her for a year."

He says, "That's right, I'm a polite person and I didn't want to interrupt her."

☺

A guy was disappointed with life and wanted to commit suicide. His friend happened to come by to visit him and sees him standing with a rope tied around his waist. The friend wondered what he was doing. The guy tells him that he's decided to commit suicide and decided to hang himself.

The friend asks, "Then why is the rope tied around your waist?"

The guy says, "I tried to tie it around my neck and almost choked."

☺

A judge asks a recalcitrant thief, "Have you ever made yourself useful to anyone in your life?"

He says, "Yes, I've given work to a few detectives, policemen, and judges."

☺

Two arrogant guys come to rent a room in a hotel. The hotel manager shows them a room that is less than the best quality.

They ask him with disdain, "How much does this pigsty cost?"

The hotel manager says, "Are you willing to take this pigsty?"

They say, "It depends on the price."

The hotel manager says, "For one pig, $100; for two pigs, $120."

☺

A girl says to her boyfriend, "I see that you've been indifferent towards me lately. When we first met you were impressed with my beauty."

He said, "That was at a masquerade party."

☺

A young couple that just got married received among the other gifts an envelope with two tickets to a play for the next week. Enclosed was a note saying, *Guess who sent this to you?*

They go to the play and keep trying to guess who sent them the tickets as a gift.

When they return home they see that burglars have emptied their home. On the table they find a note saying: *Now you know.*

☺

A woman who had been married for 40 years was asked, "How have you succeeded in being married for so long?"

The woman says, "We have an agreement. I decide on all the little things and my husband decides on all the big things."

They ask her, "What are the little things?"

She says, "For instance, what furniture to buy, what school to send the children to, which relatives to visit, where to spend our vacations, etc."

They ask her, "So what are the big things that your husband decides?"

She says, "He decides if the Americans were right to interfere in Iraq, who would make the best president, and so on."

☺

A guy who hasn't seen his girlfriend for a long time sneaks up from behind and covers her eyes.

He says, "I'll give you three tries to guess who I am. If you don't guess, I'll give you a kiss."

She says, "Churchill, Stalin, Kennedy."

☺

A guy asks his girlfriend, "Will you marry me?"

She asks, "Will you do anything I ask?"

He says, "Of course."

She asks, "Can my mother live with us?"

He says, "Of course."

She continues to ask, "Will you give me your entire salary and not ask me what I did with it?"

He says, "Of course."

She says, "I don't want to marry a person with such a lack of character."

☺

A girl asks a guy who asked her to marry him, "And if I refuse, will you go mad?"

The guy says, "Of course, that's what I always do."

☺

A guy asks his girlfriend, "Would you be willing to marry a stupid man just for his money?"

She says, "Are you doing research or are you trying to propose to me indirectly?"

☺

A man tells his friend, "I don't like my secretary. She's too organized and punctual."

The friend asks, "Why? What did she do?"

He says, "I asked her to marry me and I told her what I was willing to do for her. She typed everything word for word and an hour later gave me the paper to sign."

☺

A girl asks her father, "Does Mommy know how to take care of children?"

The father says, "Of course, sweetheart. What made you ask?"

The girl says, "Then why does she make me go to sleep when I don't want to and wake me up when I want to continue sleeping?"

☺

A girl asks her mother, "Why does the bride wear a white dress at the wedding ceremony?"

The mother says, "Because the wedding day is a day of celebration."

The girl says, "Then why does the groom wear black?"

☺

A guy asks his girlfriend, "Am I your first man?"

The girlfriend says, "Of course you're my first man. But tell me, why do all guys like to ask that question?"

☺

A husband comes home by surprise and finds his wife in bed with a strange man.

The husband says angrily, "Who is this man?"

The wife says, "That's a good question."

She turns to the man next to her and says, "What's your name?"

☺

A wife whose husband didn't come home at a very late hour sends an email to five of his friends, all of them with the same question, "Is my husband staying with you?"

The next day she gets five replies and all of his friends answered, "Yes, your husband stayed over here last night."

☺

A husband asks a man who wants to marry his daughter, "How will you provide for my daughter?"

He says, "I will have $8,000 a month."

The father says, "That's not bad, she also makes $7,000 a month."

He says, "I already included that."

☺

A single guy asks his married friend, "I don't understand why the law forbids men to marry more than one woman."

The friend says, "When you get married you'll understand that the law is there to protect men that don't know how to protect themselves."

☺

A father asks his daughter, "I heard that your boyfriend asked you to marry him?"

The daughter says, "That's right, Dad, he loves me."

The father asks, "What is his income?"

She replies, "I don't know, but that's quite a coincidence."

The father wonders, "What's the coincidence?"

The daughter says, "He also asked me what your income is."

☺

During a party the hostess asks Einstein what the relativity theory is. Einstein says that it's hard to explain. The hostess insists. Einstein says, "I'll give you an allegory:

Once a man was walking with a blind person on a hot day. The man says to the blind person, 'I would like some cold milk now.'

The blind man says, 'I know what cold is, but what is milk?'

The man says, 'Milk is a white liquid.'

The blind man says, 'I know what liquid is, but what is white?'

The man says, 'White is like the feathers of a swan.'

The blind man says, 'I know what feathers are, but what is a swan?'

The man says, 'A swan is a bird with a bent neck.'

The blind man says, 'I know what a bird is, but what is bent?'

The man takes the blind man's arm and bends it. He says, 'That is bent.'

The blind man says, 'Now I know what milk is.' "

☺

Two neighbors ran into each other at the market.

One says, "So, how's your daughter?"

The other one replies, "Thank you for asking. She's fine. She married a terrific man. He's got such a good job that she quit working at the dress shop. She doesn't have to cook because he always takes her out, and doesn't have to clean their place because he got her a housekeeper, and doesn't have to worry about my two adorable grandchildren because he got her a live-in English nanny. And your son, how is he?"

She replies, "His life is terrible. He married an awful woman. She never cooks anything and makes him take her out to dinner every night. She made him get her a maid because God forbid she should wash a dish. He has to work like crazy because she won't get a job, and she made him get her a nanny so she pays no attention to the little ones."

A woman asks her husband, "Do you love me?"
He says, "Sure."
She asks, "How much do you love me?"
He says, "How much do you need?"

A guest at a hotel was in a hurry to catch his plane. He was searching for his suitcase and couldn't find it.

He tells the bellboy, "Run quickly to my room and see if my bag is there."

The boy runs to his room, comes running back, and says to the guest, "Yes, your bag is in the room."

☺

A cop used to come visit a woman during the day when her husband wasn't home. In fear that her husband would show up unexpectedly, the woman would stand guard by the window and he would do her from behind.

One day, out of excitement, a plant fell from the rail, and the dirt and water spilled on a woman passing by in the street. The woman looked up and yelled at the woman, "You'll see, I'll send a cop to screw you."

☺

A bank manager tells a woman who is an old client that he is about to move to a different branch.

The woman says, "I'm sure that the new manager won't be as good as you."

The manager thanks her for the compliment and says politely, "How do you know? Maybe he'll be a good manager."

The woman says, "I'm sure of it. I've been doing business with this bank for thirty years and they've switched managers six times and each was worse than the one before."

☺

Two girls are playing next to the entrance of a house.

A salesman passes by and asks them, "Is Mommy home?"

The girls say, "Yes."

The salesman goes to the door and doesn't find anyone at home. He comes out angry and asks the girls, "Why did you say Mommy was home?"

The girls say, "That's not our house."

☺

A boy whose mother just put him to sleep calls to her and says, "Mommy! Bring me a glass of water."

The mother says, "I'm busy now. Go to sleep!"

The boy repeats his request.

The mother says, "If you don't go to sleep right now, you'll get a spanking."

The boy says, "When you come to spank me, bring a glass of water with you."

☺

A girl consults with her mother. She says to her, "I have a feeling that my boyfriend is going to propose to me tonight. I don't know whether to agree right away or to reject him."

The mother says, "If you see that he's too excited, tell him that you want to think about it, and if you see that he asks you hesitantly, say yes immediately before he changes his mind."

☺

A husband tells his wife that he heard from the postman that he'd slept with all the women in the building except for one and asks her if that's possible.

His wife says, "Yes, I know her, she's the crazy woman from apartment 6A."

☺

A large shoe factory sent two salesmen to Africa to check out if there is potential there for marketing shoes. One of the salesmen was a pessimist and the other an optimist.

After two weeks, the pessimist reports that there's no chance to market shoes because everyone goes barefoot. The optimist reports that there's a good market there for shoes because nobody has any.

☺

During the funeral of a ninety-year-old millionaire, a man is standing at the side weeping bitterly.

Somebody goes up to him to comfort him and asks him, "Who was this man to you? Was he a relative?"

The man says, "No, he wasn't my relative, that's why I'm crying."

☺

A boy asks his father, "Why can't you give me money to go on a trip with my friends?"

The father says, "Because!"

The son says, " 'Because' is no answer."

The father asks, "Why isn't 'Because' an answer?"

The boy says, "Because!"

☺

A guy goes to the psychiatrist with a cigarette in his nose, a string of gum around his neck, dragging a shoe tied to a string behind him.

The psychiatrist asks him, "What is your problem?"

The guy said, "It's not me, I came for my friend. Lately he's been scratching his right ear with his left hand and he refuses to see a psychiatrist."

☺

A woman says to her neighbor, "You look very pretty today."

The neighbor says, "It's a pity I can't say the same for you."

The woman says, "Why can't you? You could lie, too."

☺

An angry woman comes to the vegetable store and says to the greengrocer, "These apples that you sold me are rotten. Look, they have worms."

The greengrocer says, "Ma'am, these apples are so delicious that even the worms love them."

☺

A husband and wife weren't speaking to each other and they would correspond through notes.

One evening the husband gives a note to his wife saying, *Wake me up at 6:00 in the morning.*

The next day, the man wakes up on his own, looks at the clock and sees that it's already 10:00. He gets angry that his wife didn't wake him.

He gets out of bed and finds a note next to the bed saying, *It's 6:00 now, you have to get up.*

☺

Three people are walking in a park and each one is pulling a string with a bottle tied to the end.

A man passing by asked each of them, "What are you pulling around a bottle for?"

Two of them say, "It's my dog and I'm taking it for a walk."

The third says, "It's my bottle."

The man says to the third one, "I can see that you're normal, what are you doing with those other two?"

The third one says, "You're right, I shouldn't be with them."

After the man leaves, the third one says to his bottle, "You see, Maxi, we fooled him. Now he believes that you're a bottle."

☺

A guy that just got married was having marriage troubles. Every morning he would go to synagogue and after his prayers he would stand in front of the Holy Ark and spill his heart out to God, asking, "When, when will my troubles end?"

The caretaker got tired of him. One morning the caretaker hid behind the Ark's curtain.

When the guy repeated the question, "When, when will my troubles end?"

The caretaker answers in a deep whisper, "In a year."

The guy gets excited that God answered and he asks what will happen in a year.

The voice answers, "In a year, you'll get used to your troubles."

☺

A girl asks her boyfriend, "Who do you think has better taste, me or you?"

The boyfriend says to her, "You have better taste."

She asks, "How did you decide that?"

He says, "You chose me and I chose you."

☺

The judge doesn't believe the defendant and says to her, "You know what a person who lies on trial is destined to?"

She says, "Yes, sir, my lawyer told me."

The judge says, "What did the lawyer tell you?"

She says, "He told me that if I lie I'll have a chance to save myself from punishment."

☺

Two clerks are sitting in the office lunchroom during their break. One is tense and drinks his coffee quickly and takes a bite of his sandwich. He wants to finish and leave, and the other sits calmly, drinks a sip and stops, looks at the newspaper and takes another sip. The tense one says that he's very overloaded with work and has a pile of letters on his desk waiting for him to take care of and asks the calm one, "How do you have so much time?"

The calm one says, "I have my own method of handling the letters. Every time I get a letter I write on it: *Please pass on to Steve.* I'm sure that in such a big office there must be at least one person named Steve."

The tense one gets up and punches the calm one.

The calm one asks, "What was that about? What have I done to you?"

The tense one says, "I'm Steve."

☺

During an argument in court the judge says to the lawyer, "Go outside with the defendant and give him some good advice on how to get out of this mess."

The lawyer goes out with the defendant and a minute later returns alone.

The judge says, "Where's the defendant?"

The lawyer says, "He ran away. That was the best advice I could give him."

☺

A salesman tells his friend, "Yesterday afternoon I came home early and found my wife on the couch with my business partner."

The friend says, "You must be planning to divorce your wife."

The salesman says, "No, my wife is an excellent housekeeper. I couldn't get along without her."

The friend says, "Then you must be planning on leaving your partner."

The salesman says, "No, my partner brought most of the investment to the business."

The friend says, "So, aren't you going to do anything?"

The salesman says, "Sure I am, I'm going to sell the couch."

☺

A football player who was known to be a modest person said in his testimony at a trial that he's the best player in the country.

After the trial his coach asked him, "How can you say something like that about yourself? You always tell your friends on the team that there are better players than you."

The player says, "In court I had to tell the truth."

☺

A member of the Board of Education visits a school.

He goes into one classroom and sees that they're having a lesson on sex.

He goes into another classroom and sees that there too they're having a lesson on sex.

He's on his way to see the principal and meets two students, a girl and a boy, sitting in the hallway kissing.

He asks them, "Why aren't you in class?"

They say, "We're doing our homework together."

☺

A man goes to visit the doctor.

The doctor examines him and asks, "Have you seen another doctor before me?"

The man says, "I haven't been to another doctor but I've been to the pharmacist."

The doctor asks, "And what idiotic advice did he give you?"

The man says, "He advised me to go see you."

☺

A teacher punishes two pupils who broke the same rule to write their names one hundred times on the blackboard after class.

One of the students says, "But that's not fair, teacher. His name is Eli and my name is Alexander."

☺

Three people are sitting playing cards.

One says, "I get the money because I have two kings."

The second one says, "I have two aces so I get the money."

The third one says, "I only have two tens but I also have two guns."

They let him have the money.

☺

A young king visits an airplane factory and sees that one of the workers looks a lot like him.

He says to the worker, "Maybe your mother used to work at the palace when my father was king?"

The worker says, "My mother didn't work in the palace, but my father was a gardener there."

☺

A married man complains to his friend about his wife who never agrees with him and always says 'No'.

The friend says, "Doesn't she ever say 'Yes'?"

The man says, "Only once."

The friend asks, "When was that?"

The man says, "When we got married."

☺

A father buys a watch for his son at the store and asks to have his son's name engraved on it.

The shop owner says, "You must be intending to surprise your son."

The father says, "Of course, and what a surprise. He's expecting me to buy him a car."

☺

During the Communist era, an American and a Russian had a race. The American came in first.

A Russian reporter, afraid to report the American's victory, wrote a piece for his newspaper that read: *In a race that was held today, the Russian came in second and the American came in one before last.*

☺

A schoolteacher has her students write an essay on "Mother: There is Only One" and asks that the essay be short and include an event that justifies the title name. One pupil, who wasn't very bright, gets the idea. Two weeks later he hands in an essay that reads:

One day I came home from school. I was very hungry. I asked my mother, "What is there to eat?"

She says, "I made the muffins that you like."

I said, "I don't want them."

She said, "I could make you an omelet with two eggs."

I said, "Okay."

She said, "Sweetie, get me two eggs from the refrigerator."

I opened the refrigerator and saw only one egg.

I said, "Mother, there is only one."

☺

A husband complained to his friend, "My wife is always asking for more and more money."

The friend says, "And what does she do with all that money?"

The husband says, "I don't know. I haven't given her any yet."

☺

A chronic drunk is accepted to a rehabilitation center. In order to demonstrate that drinking is damaging to your health, they put two glasses in front of him.

One contains water, the other vodka. They put a worm in each glass. The worm in the glass of water floats with pleasure whereas the worm in the glass of vodka dies.

They ask him, "What did you learn from this?"

The drunk says, "I learned that if you drink vodka, you'll never have worms."

☺

During an agriculture class the teacher asks, "What's the best time for picking fruit?"

One of the students says, "When the guard's asleep."

☺

A judge warns a witness who's about to testify, "You must only say things that you know from your personal experience and not from hearsay."

The witness says, "I understand, Your Honor."

The judge says, "Alright. First, tell me, where were you born?"

The witness says, "I can't tell you, I know that only by hearsay."

☺

A man meets his neighbor in the mall.

He says to her, "You like sex in a threesome?"

She says, "If one of them is my husband, sure I do."

He says, "If you run home quickly, you might still make it."

☺

A new manager in a bank invites a few of his clients to hear what they do.

An elegant woman comes in.

He asks her, "What do you do?"

She says, "I make bets. I'm willing to bet you $500 that in a week your willy will be square."

The manager is sure that this won't happen. He agrees to the bet.

A week later, she returns to the bank and he shows her.

She says, "I bet $1,000 with someone else that in a week you'd show me your willy."

☺

A woman goes to a gynecologist's clinic. She sees two men in white coats. She gets undressed.

The first one approaches, spreads her legs, and looks.

He says, "That's really something."

He suggests to the other that he take a look, too.

He looks and also says, "That's really something."

She says, "What's something? What do I have there?"

The men say, "We don't know. We came to paint the walls."

☺

A man goes to the doctor complaining of amnesia.

He says, "I forget everything I've done even if it was just a few minutes ago."

The doctor says, "Well, first put $100 on the table before you forget why you came here today."

☺

There was a man who was as ugly as a monkey but was very righteous. No woman wanted him. One day he wins $2,000,000 in the lottery. The man goes to a plastic surgeon and says, "I want you to make me good looking."

The doctor says, "My friend, this will be very difficult. Nothing is in the right place with you. I'll have to perform a few operations, but it's possible. It will cost you $1,000,000."

The man says, "I'm willing."

The doctor works on him for a few months and makes him into a good-looking man. The man buys some modern clothes and with his head held high goes out to see how the women react.

A car passes by and runs him over. He goes to heaven.

He says, "I want to see the angel in charge of life."

They bring him before the angel.

The man says, "You know I was a very righteous man, why did you take me?"

The angel says, "Oh, it's you! I'm sorry I didn't recognize you!!!"

☺

A worker in a factory that manufactured construction materials would leave the factory at the end of his workday with a sack full of remnants that were to be thrown away. By his behavior, the guard suspected that he was stealing something.... maybe he was hiding something in the sack. The guard decided to check the content of the sack a few times and found nothing. But his instincts as a guard told him that the worker was stealing something.

Thirty years later after they'd both retired, they meet again.

The guard says to the worker, "I always suspected that you were stealing something. Now that everything's over you can tell me what you stole."

The worker says, "Sacks."

☺

A farmer in a country ruled by a dictator wants to be accepted to the ruling party.

The secretary asks him, "If you're asked to give your truck to the party, will you agree?"

The farmer says, "Of course."

The secretary continues, asking, "And if you're asked to give your horse to the party?"

The farmer says, "Sure."

The secretary continues, "And if you're asked to donate your cow?"

The farmer says, "Not my cow."

The secretary says, "You're willing to give up your truck and your horse but not your cow? Why not?"

The farmer says, "Because I actually have a cow."

☺

A little boy sits in his room playing with his toys. He tries to build a tower.

His father comes into the room, sees what he's trying to do, and goes to help him.

The boy says, "Don't bother me, go play with your newspaper."

☺

The people of Chelm, who were known for their remarkable lack of intelligence, discussed the question of how to greet the Messiah when he arrives. If he arrives on a weekday, they thought, people will be busy with their work, some will be wearing dirty work clothes, others will be in the middle of doing laundry or cleaning.

They sought advice and decided to build a tower at the city entrance and to post a guard there. When the guard sees the Messiah coming near on his donkey, the guard was to tell the townspeople so they could prepare.

Everything is set according to the plan. When the guard comes down from the tower on Friday, they ask him, "How's your new job?"

He says, "What can I say? It's boring up there alone and the pay is lousy, but it's a job that will last a lifetime."

☺

Three hookers are brought before a judge.

The judge asks the first one, "What is your occupation?"

She says, "I'm a teacher."

The judge asks the second one the same question and she too says that she's a teacher.

The judge asks the third one. She says, "I'm a hooker."

He asks her, "How's business these days?"

The hooker says, "Not too good, there are a lot of teachers roaming around the streets lately."

☺

A policeman stops a woman driver who ran a red light.

He says, "License and registration, please."

She says, "I don't have a driver's license, a car registration, or insurance."

The policeman goes to his sergeant sitting in the car.

The sergeant comes over and says to her, "Where's your license, registration, and proof of insurance?"

She hands him a driver's license, car registration, and insurance card.

The sergeant says to the policeman, "Why did you tell me she didn't have any license and registration?"

The driver tells the sergeant, "You see what a liar he is? Soon he'll tell you that I ran a red light."

☺

A professor had to get to a small island. He rents a fisherman's boat.

On the way the professor asks the fisherman, "Did you study mathematics?"

The fisherman says, "I haven't."

The professor says, "You missed out on a big part of your life."

They continue to sail. The professor asks him, "Have you studied philosophy?"

The fisherman says, "No, I haven't."

The professor says, "You missed out on another big part of your life."

They continue to sail. Suddenly a storm hits. The boat turns over.

The fisherman asks the professor, "Have you learned how to swim?"

The professor says, "No, I haven't."

The fisherman says, "You missed out on your entire life."

☺

After finishing his dinner at a restaurant, a man asks for the bill.

The waitress gives him the bill for $19.80.

The man gives her $20 and waits for the change.

She doesn't come back.

He asks, "What about the change?"

She brings him 20 cents and a condom in a plate.

He asks, "What's the condom for?"

She says, "I don't want people like you to reproduce."

☺

A teacher asks his students what organ in the human body increases to eight times its size when excited. There is silence in the classroom. Nobody answers.

The teacher approaches one girl and asks what she thinks. She blushes, giggles and doesn't answer.

The teacher says, "First of all, it's the human pupil of the eye. Second, you should know that you're in for a big disappointment on your wedding night."

☺

A priest asks his Jewish friend to take his place for a week when he's on vacation.

The Jew says, "I don't know exactly what to do."

The priest says, "It's quite simple. You sit in the confession booth. People come to you and confess their sins. You tell them what prayers to say for atonement. Here is the penance list."

The Jew agrees. The Jew sits in the booth.

One man comes to him and says, "Father, I have sinned, I've betrayed my wife."

The Jew looks at the list and says, "One hundred Hail Mary's."

A woman comes and says, "I've betrayed my husband."

He looks at the list and says, "Two hundred Our Father's."

Afterwards a guy comes and says, "I have sinned. I let a girl give me a blowjob in the bathroom."

The Jew can't find the sin on the list.

He goes to the kitchen and asks one of the nuns how much the priest gives for a blowjob in the bathroom.

She says, "A chocolate bar."

☺

A foolish guy marries a salesman's daughter.

Three months later she tells him, "I have labor pains, take me to the hospital."

He says, "How can that be? We've only been married for three months."

She says, "Look, I've been married for three months and you've been married for three months, that's six."

He says, "What about the other three months?"

She says, "For three months we've both been married."

He says, "And that's the correct calculation. Come, I'll take you to the hospital."

☺

A guy meets his friend on the street.

The friend says, "I heard you have a small organ."

The guy says, "I knew that Emily had a big mouth."

☺

A woman says to her friend, "I don't know what to do. My husband is such a mess maker that you can't imagine. He doesn't put anything in its place, I'm always going around the house organizing things."

The friend says, "Take a tip from me. The first week after we were married I told him firmly, 'Every glass and plate that you take, wash when you are done and put it back in its place.' "

The woman says, "Well, did it help?"

The friend says, "I don't know. Since then he disappeared."

☺

A man goes into a store that sells all kinds of accessories and asks for a disguise.

The salesman says, "Over there, in the corner, at the end of the store."

The man goes over, looks around, comes back and says, "I didn't find it."

The salesman goes with him, sees that he ran out of stock, and says, "Wow! Our disguises are so good that both of us can't see them. We have a special expert for seeing them. Come back next week and he'll be here."

☺

A man was suspicious that his wife was cheating on him but he always had doubts. One day he had to go out of town and he asked his son to follow his mother and report back to him.

When the man comes back a few days later, he asks his son, "So, did you see anything?"

The son says, "Nothing special. In the evening, someone that I don't know came to visit Mom. They went into the bedroom. I peeked through the keyhole."

The father says impatiently, "So, what did you see?"

He says, "I saw them undressing."

The father says, "So, what else did you see?"

The son says, "Afterwards I couldn't see anything because they turned out the light."

The father says, "Oh, those doubts, those doubts are killing me!"

☺

A man and woman sit on a park bench and make out.

A policeman comes over and asks them, "Are you married?"

They say, "Yes."

He says, "Go home and fool around in private. Why should you do it in public?"

The man says, "We can't."

The policeman asks, "Why?"

The man says, "My wife's at home and her husband's at home."

☺

A dictator and a democratic president meet.

The dictator asks the president, "Do you have a hobby?"

The president says, "Yes, I collect the jokes that are told about me."

The president asks the dictator, "And do you have a hobby?"

The dictator says, "Yes, I collect the people that tell jokes about me."

☺

A shepherd was in a field with a herd of cows. A man comes with a notebook in his hand and says to the shepherd, "Your cows look very healthy, what do you feed them?"

The shepherd says, "I don't know, anything that's in the field, grass, thorns, scraps of food."

The man says, "I'm from the organization for prevention of cruelty to animals. I'm charging you a $100 fine for being cruel to cows."

The next day the shepherd goes out with the herd again.

Another man comes with a notebook in his hand and says, "Your cows look very healthy, what do you feed them?"

The shepherd says, "I give them bread, meat and fruit."

The man says, "How dare you waste that kind of food on cows when there are so many hungry people! I'm charging you a $200 fine."

The next day the shepherd goes out to the field with the herd again. Again a man comes with a notebook in his hand. He says, "You have healthy cows, what do you feed them?"

The shepherd says, "Every morning I give each of them $5 to go and buy whatever they want."

☺

A man who was married to the same woman for 30 years comes home by surprise one day and finds his wife in bed with his best friend.

He looks at his friend in astonishment and says, "I have to, but you?!"

☺

A man who worked in Paris for a number of years comes back to his homeland.

His wife says, "Let's go to a hotel to celebrate your return."

After a hearty meal with a bottle of wine, they go to sleep in their room. Early in the morning, one of the hotel workers knocks on the door. They're both drowsy.

The man jumps up and says, "That must be your husband!"

She says, "It can't be, my husband's in Paris."

☺

A man sits next to a woman on a train.

The woman says, "I'm very cold. Maybe you could go ask the conductor for a blanket for me."

The man says, "Let's act as if we're married."

She likes the idea and agrees.

He says, "If you're already my wife, then go ask for the blanket yourself."

☺

A diplomat arrives in a country where he doesn't understand the language. One day, he's invited to speak at a meeting of the local actors' union. The head stage manager is translating what he says.

The diplomat remembers what he learned in a public speaking course, that you should begin a speech with a joke, so he starts to tell a joke. He takes a long time, getting into the details.

When he's finished the stage manager says one short sentence and everyone laughs.

The diplomat is surprised, and asks the stage manager, "How did you translate all that into one sentence?"

The stage manager says, "Very simple. I said that our guest told a joke, now everybody laugh."

☺

A woman goes to a marriage counselor and complains about two problems she has. One problem is that she has 8 children and they wear her out. The second problem is that her husband doesn't love her.

The marriage counselor says, "Imagine how many children you'd have if your husband did love you."

☺

A woman complains to her mother that her husband doesn't have sex with her.

The mother says, "That's hard for me to believe. I want to peek to see if it's true."

The daughter agrees.

At night, the mother peeks. She sees the husband sitting in bed reading a book and the daughter lying beside him. A while later he puts his finger in her vagina.

The mother says to herself, 'If he put his finger inside that means that he will continue."

The next day she tells her daughter, "I peeked last night and I saw him put his finger inside you, that means everything is okay."

The daughter says, "It's not what you think, when he wants to turn the page he puts his finger in there."

☺

Roger was in a terrible car accident, which mangled his willy and tore it from his body. His doctor assures him that modern medicine could give him back his manhood, but that he would have to pay personally to have this done, this kind of surgery was not covered entirely by his medical insurance. Roger tells the doctor that it was not going to be a problem. This was so important, he would pay for it out of his savings.

"So how much will it cost?" asks Roger.

The doctor says, "$10,000 for a small one, $15,000 for medium, and $25,000 for large."

Roger says, "Okay, I'd like the large one, please."

But the doctor urges him to talk it over with his wife before making such an important decision, and leaves the room to allow Roger to call his wife on his cell phone.

Roger spends ten minutes discussing his options with Lisa, and when the doctor comes back into the room, he finds Roger looking miserable.

"Well, what have the two of you decided?" asks the doctor.

Roger answers, "Lisa said she'd rather have a new kitchen."

☺

A group of soldiers arrives late to a guidance class. The first one goes in.

The commander asks, "Why are you late?"

The soldier said, "I was waiting for a ride. A horse and carriage stopped for me. I felt uncomfortable refusing a man who wanted to do me a favor. You know that a carriage doesn't go as fast as a car."

The second soldier goes in and tells the same story that the carriage stopped for him. The same goes on with the third, and the fourth.

The last soldier goes in. The commander says, "So, the carriage probably stopped for you, too."

The soldier says, "No, actually a new car stopped for me, but the road was full of horses and carriages."

☺

A guy who goes on a trip with his girlfriend writes to his father that he needs $2,000.

The father sends him $200 and in the letter he writes, *Allow me to correct an error you made. Two hundred is written with two zeros, not three.*

☺

During a party, a lawyer and a doctor stand in a corner talking. Every few minutes one of the guests would go over to the doctor and ask for his advice on some problem.

The doctor says, "I don't know what to do, there are always annoying people that don't leave me alone with their medical questions when I'm out at a social gathering."

The lawyer says, "I'll tell you what to do. Every time somebody asks me for advice, I give it to him patiently. The next day I send him a bill."

The doctor caught on to the idea. He sends out bills.

A week later he goes to check his mailbox to see how many letters he got with checks. He finds one letter. He opens it and finds a bill from the lawyer who gave him the advice.

☺

A tourist visited the Capitol in Washington and was looking for a garbage can in the hallway.

When he didn't find one, he asked a congressman that passed by, "How come there's no garbage can here?"

The congressman, who was known for his sense of humor, says, "We don't need one here. The Republicans throw their garbage at the Democrats, and the Democrats throw their garbage at the Republicans, and the reporters take it all out."

☺

A girl sits in the park eating a piece of cake. Her friend comes and sits down next to her. He looks at her cake with envy.

He says, "It's too bad nobody gave me a piece of cake like that."

She asks, "Why?"

He says, "I would have given you half."

The girl doesn't get the hint. She continues to eat the cake.

When she's finished she says, "It's really too bad that no one gave you cake like that. I would have happily taken the half that you would have offered me."

☺

A lawyer goes hunting with his friend. They shoot a mountain goat.

The friend says, "You watch the mountain goat and I'll go get two friends to help us pick it up."

The friend comes back an hour later and sees that the mountain goat disappeared.

He asks, "Where's the mountain goat?"

The lawyer says, "What mountain goat?"

The friend says, "We went hunting, right?"

The lawyer says, "Right."

The friend says, "We shot a mountain goat, right?"

The lawyer says, "Right."

The friend continues, "And I told you to stay here and watch the mountain goat, right?"

The lawyer says, "Right."

The friend asks, "Then where is the mountain goat?"

The lawyer says, "What mountain goat?"

☺

A guy sits down at the bar in a nightclub. Near him a girl is sitting alone.

He says, "Can I buy you a drink?"

She says, "I don't drink."

He says, "Do you want to go for a walk?"

She says, "I don't like to go for walks."

He says, "Maybe you'd like to come home with me to listen to music?"

She says, "I don't like music."

He says, "Well, then, there's probably no use in talking about going to bed together."

☺

During a flight a stewardess sees a man with a tag on his shirt with the letters 'N.C.' The stewardess asks him what those initials stand for.

The man says, "They stand for Nymphomaniacs Conference. I'm returning from the conference."

She asks him, "What, for instance, did you discuss?"

He says, "One of the topics we discussed was the question of what girls prefer, the South American's big organ or the Jew's witty mind."

She says, "That is really interesting."

He says, "Which do you prefer?"

She says, "First tell me your name."

He says, "Alejandro Rabinowitz."

☺

There were two lines at the entrance to heaven. One line for men who obeyed their wives and the second line for men who stood up for their opinions. The first line was long. Only one man stood on the second line.

An angel came up to him and said, "Good for you, you're saving the male honor. Tell me exactly how you came to stand on this line."

The man says, "I don't know, my wife told me to stand here."

☺

Two women at a senior home are discussing their ambitions that hadn't materialized.

One says, "I've always wanted to go out naked on the street and drive the guys crazy."

The second says, "I wanted to do that, too. Why don't we do it now?"

They undress and go outside. Two old men are sitting at the entrance of the building.

After they pass by one says to the other, "Who were they? It was hard to make out the color of their dresses."

The second says, "You're right it was hard, but one thing's for sure, their dresses weren't ironed."

☺

At an army base, Master Sergeant Berkowitz was in charge of the kitchen. One day, the base commander tells Berkowitz that in two days the Major General will be coming to visit.

Berkowitz says, "He's a friend of mine, I know him well."

The commander is doubtful. When the Major General arrives, he goes straight over to Berkowitz and shakes his hand. The commander is surprised.

Berkowitz says, "All the important people are friends of mine."

A week later, the Chief of Staff comes, then the Head of Security, they both speak on friendly terms with Berkowitz.

The commander says to Berkowitz, "Next week my deputy and I will be going to Rome, come with us. If you prove that you know the Pope then I'll be convinced that you know all the important people."

Berkowitz says, "No problem."

The three of them arrive at the Vatican. Berkowitz disappears for half an hour and appears with the Pope on the balcony. When Berkowitz gets back, he sees that the commander passed out.

He asks his deputy, "What happened to the commander?"

The deputy says, "There were two tourists from China here. When you and the Pope appeared on the balcony, one of the Chinese men asked the commander, "Tell me, who's that man next to Berkowitz?"

A man tells his friend, "I have a problem with my wife. She doesn't like sex so I visit my girlfriend in the evening. When I get back late, I park the car far from the house, open the door quietly and tiptoe to bed, but my wife wakes up anyway."

The friend says, "Take my advice. My wife doesn't like sex, either. When I get home, I park next to the house, come in noisily, turn on the light, get into bed and start to stroke her, and she pretends to be asleep."

A monk and a soldier stand on the road and try to hitch a ride.

A car stops and the driver says, "Just the soldier can come."

The monk says, "What kind of discrimination is this? Why can the soldier come and I can't?"

The driver says, "The soldier serves his country."

The monk says, "And I serve God."

The driver says, "So let God give you a lift."

☺

A woman who doesn't like sex comes home one day and sees her husband masturbating.

She says, "Wait, honey, stop! I'll be right back."

The husband says, "What happened? You suddenly feel like having sex?"

She says, "No, let me go get a towel so you don't dirty the carpet."

☺

A man who was thought to be righteous arrives in heaven. He goes straight to heaven's gates.

The angel on duty looks in his file and says, "You were righteous but you sinned by looking down a woman's neckline twice, as punishment you will get an ugly partner for eternity."

Suddenly a very ugly well-known criminal passes by with a pretty partner.

The man says to the angel, "What justice is this? Why did he get such a pretty girl?"

The angel says, "He's her punishment."

☺

Mrs. Jones from London was visiting some friends in Florida when she saw a little old man rocking merrily away on his front porch. He had a lovely smile on his face. She just had to go over to him.

"I couldn't help noticing how happy you look. I would love to know your secret for a long and happy life," says Mrs. Jones.

The man stops rocking, looks at her and smiles. He says, "I'll tell you since you asked. I smoke four packs of cigarettes a day, drink five bottles of whiskey a week, eat lots and lots of fatty food, and I never, I mean *never*, exercise."

"Why, that's absolutely amazing!" exclaims Mrs. Jones. "I've never heard anything like this before. How old are you?"

He replies, "I'm twenty-six."

☺

A man had a few beehives in his backyard. One day a bee comes into his bathroom and stings him on the tip of his willy. The area gets swollen. His wife takes him to the doctor.

The doctor says, "I'll give you medicine that will heal the area."

The wife says, "Maybe you have medicine that will keep it swollen?"

☺

John and his friend take a trip to Sweden. When they're in the countryside at night their car breaks down and they spend the night with an old woman living alone in a villa.

In the middle of the night, John disappears for two hours and goes to visit the woman. In fear of being found out, he gives his friend's name and address when she asks how to contact him.

Two years later the friend tells John, "Yesterday I got a message that a Swedish woman left me a million dollar inheritance. It must be the woman we stayed with. I wonder how she got my address."

☺

Two women are sitting in a hotel lobby and complaining about the hotel's terrible conditions.

One says, "They don't know how to cook, the food tastes bland."

The second one says, "And the portions are small, and if you ask for a second helping they don't give it to you."

☺

A man goes to a lawyer and tells him what the problem is.

The lawyer says, "I'll take your case, I'm sure you'll win the trial."

The man says, "I won't go to trial."

He asks him, "Why not?"

The man says, "I just told you the other side's story."

☺

A doctor has a fight with his wife. When he's about to leave the house, he stops by the door and says, "I want to tell you one more thing. You're not so great in bed."

When he comes back home he finds his wife in bed with a strange man.

He says, "What's this about?"

She says, "I wanted to get a second opinion."

☺

A woman, who didn't like her husband taking Viagra, stole his medication and threw it in the toilet.

Ever since then they can't close the lid.

☺

An atheist says to a religious man, "Both of us won't get to go to heaven."

The religious man says, "On what do you base this idea?"

The atheist says, "I won't go because I'm an atheist and I don't deserve heaven. And you won't go because heaven doesn't exist."

☺

A congregant asked his priest, "Father, you're a man of God. So why is it that you are always talking business when I, a businessman, am always talking about spiritual matters when I'm not at work?"

"You have discovered one of the principles of human nature," the priest replied.

"And what principle is that?" asked the man.

"People like to discuss things they know nothing about."

☺

A grandmother goes for a walk in the park with her grandson.

Her friend meets her and says, "What a nice grandson you have."

The grandmother says, "Oh, that's nothing, you should see his picture."

☺

Two friends are complaining about life.

One of them sighs and says to the other, "Considering how hard life is, death isn't such a bad thing. In fact, I think sometimes it's better not to have been born at all."

"True," says his friend. "But how many men are that lucky? Maybe one in ten thousand!"

☺

A man calls his friend to wish him a Happy New Year.

The friend says, "Is that you? I read an obituary about you in the newspaper today. Where are you calling from?"

☺

In a contest for the best-looking man, three men are chosen. First place, second place, and third place.

The host says to the man who won third place, "You get a Cadillac."

The man that won second place gets on the stage, the host tells him, "You won a big cheesecake."

The man says, "How can you give the third place a Cadillac and the second place just a cake?"

The host says, "It's a special cake. It was made by Madonna herself."

The man says angrily, "Madonna?! Let her kiss my ass."

The host says, "That's the prize for the first place winner."

☺

A teacher is walking in the schoolyard. He sees a group of children sitting in a circle in the corner playing with something.

He goes up to them and asks them, "What are you playing with?"

They tell him, "We're having a contest: who can tell the biggest lie, and we even have a chocolate bar as a prize."

The teacher says, "This game isn't educational. When I was your age, I never lied."

All the children say, "The prize is yours!"

☺

A man tells his friend, "After forty years of marriage, my wife and I finally agree about sex."

The friend says, "Really? You always said that your wife doesn't like sex. What happened all of a sudden?"

The man says, "That's right, she still doesn't like it but now I don't need it anymore."

☺

A guy invites a girl to dinner at his house. After dinner he tries to get her into bed. All his efforts are failing. Finally he loses his patience. He asks her directly, "Don't you understand what I want?"

She says, "Why don't you give me a hint?"

He pulls down his pants and shows her his willy.

She says, "No, that hint is too small."

☺

A woman sits next to her husband's bed in the hospital. He tells her about the surgery he had and says that he's very worried.

She says, "Don't worry, I'm sure you'll get out of bed healthy and in one piece."

He asks her, "How can you be so sure?"

She says, "Look, we owe $2,000 to the doctor, $400 to the nurse and another $2,500 to the hospital. The way these people are, they won't let you die."

☺

A man comes to the doctor and complains that his wife doesn't hear well and refuses to go to the doctor. He asks him to give her a hearing aid.

The doctor says, "From what distance can't she hear?"

The man says, "I don't know, I didn't measure."

The doctor says, "Go measure. I can't fit a hearing aid for her without it."

The man goes home, asks his wife from six feet away, "What's for lunch?"

The woman doesn't answer.

He gets closer and from four feet away, he asks again.

She doesn't answer.

He gets closer, and from two feet away, again asks, "What's for lunch?"

She says, "Fish, fish, fish! I've told you twice already!"

☺

A married couple was married for 25 years.

A friend of the family asks the husband, "What gift are you thinking of getting your wife for your anniversary?"

The husband says, "I'm planning on sending her to China with her mother."

The friend says, "That's a very nice gift. If you give her such a big gift for your 25th anniversary, then what gift will you get her for your 50th wedding anniversary?"

The husband says, "Then I'll bring her back from China."

Afterword

There's a joke from which I learned some of life's wisdom. I opened the book with this joke and I would like to end it with the same joke. As you know, most of the arguments between people are arguments in vain, i.e., it doesn't matter to you at all if the other side agrees with your opinion. Sometimes when I'm in the middle of an argument with someone I'll remember this joke, and then with no connection to what I've said earlier, or what he has said, I'll suddenly say, "You're right."

Not only don't you lose anything, you gain sympathy and save nerves. And this is the joke:

A man meets his friend after he hadn't seen him in twenty years. He says to his friend, "You look terrific! What do you do to look so good?"

The friend says, "Look, I have one rule. I don't argue with people."

The man says, "How can it be from that?!"

The friend says, "You're right, it couldn't possibly be from that."